To Shubha Chacko and to Balwant Singh
—P.G.

Collection Editors:

Laure Mistral
Philippe Godard

Also Available:

We Live in China

We Live in

India

भारत

By Philippe Godard

Illustrations by
Sophie Duffet

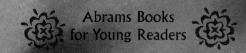

Abrams Books
for Young Readers

Because this is a book for young readers, I would like to offer them not a preface, but a testimonial—a tribute to the Indian kids whom I had the great fortune to meet in Calcutta and, more personally, in an especially destitute shantytown in that immense metropolis. They are the true source of the Indian spirit.

Their neighborhood is called the City of Joy. Here, children rule. Their carefree attitude, the joy they take simply in existing, their magical smiles, their somber faces pierced by the penetrating light of their glances—all of this sets off, with improbable splendor, the dismal universe where they've had the misfortune to be born. Without these children, this dilapidated district would be nothing more than a hard-labor camp.

In a small communal courtyard, a squalid recess measuring a few square yards that almost never got any sunlight, I counted sixty-two children.

That's where they attend the pitiless school of life, as they learn to survive by themselves from their earliest childhoods.

The years spent at play are incredibly fleeting for the young girls of the City of Joy. Starting when they're six or seven, they're in charge of all of the household chores—even the most thankless ones. From morning to night, they go smiling about their work as future homemakers. In fact, their entire education is meant to point them toward their final goal and crowning achievement: marriage. Their mothers invest all their energy in teaching them everything they'll need to know to become model wives and mothers.

For young Indians from such deprived neighborhoods, school—real school—is, unfortunately, a dream that's almost totally denied to them. When they're seven or eight, the children of the City of Joy must leave their games behind and drop out of school to help guarantee the survival of their families. They have to work. An extra salary, even a small fraction of a salary, can mean an additional meal. Perhaps they'll make household utensils or pens, roll cigarettes, or produce matches, as they spend ten or twelve hours a day in a workshop, deprived of nearly all light and air. For these kids, there are no vacations or weekends.

Fortunately, though, not all Indian children are doomed to cope with the adversity of the slum districts that disfigure India's major cities. More than one hundred million children attend real schools, technical institutes, and advanced universities. They're lucky enough to receive an education with which they can build the largest democracy in the world.

—Dominique Lapierre

Dominique Lapierre is the author of several books about India, including *Freedom at Midnight*, *The City of Joy*, and *Five Past Midnight in Bhopal*. One half of the royalties he earns is donated to the Program for Assistance to the Children of Lepers in Calcutta.

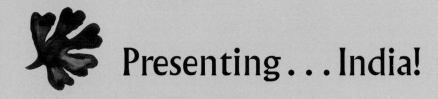

Presenting ... India!

Surface Area: 1,270,000 square miles.

Population: 1,027,000,000 people, according to the 2001 census. India is the second most populous country in the world, after China (with 1.3 billion inhabitants), and is well ahead of the third most populous nation, the United States (297 million people).

Population Density: With 808 inhabitants per square mile, many times the population density of the U.S., India is home to 16.7 percent of the world's population living on 2.4 percent of the earth's land surface, thus making it one of the largest population centers on the planet.

Major Languages: Hindi, Punjabi, Urdu, Marathi, and Gujarati are spoken in the north and west, Bengali in the northeast, and Tamil, Kannada, Malayalam, and Telugu in the southern and central regions. There are 18 official languages in India, and about 1,500 languages and dialects.

Indian Religions include Hinduism (about 85 percent of the people), Islam (12 percent), Christianity (2.3 percent), Panth (Sikhism, 2 percent), Buddhism (0.7 percent), Jainism (0.5 percent) and Zoroastrianism (religion of the Parsis), as well as the religions of the "tribes," that is, the descendants of the first peoples to settle in India.

India's Main Cities:
Bombay: 16.3 million people
Delhi: 13.8 million people
Calcutta: 13.2 million people
Madras: 4.2 million people
Bangalore: 4.1 million people
(Officially, Bombay, Calcutta, and Madras are now known
as Mumbai, Kolkata, and Chennai, respectively.)

India Is a Vast Asian Nation: The seventh largest country in the world, India lies in isolation. To the west, south, and east, there is ocean. To the north, the Himalaya mountain range cuts it off from the rest of Asia. It's as though the country is a whole continent in itself, sheltering its extremely diverse peoples, languages, and customs in its various regions. India is divided into states. Some, like Uttar Pradesh in the north, have extremely large populations (Uttar Pradesh has 166 million people). The Indian currency is called the rupee, and it is divided into 100 paise.

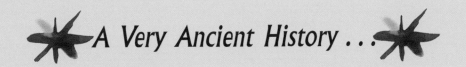

A Very Ancient History . . .

The oldest Indian city, now submerged in the sea, is 7,000 years old. Some archaeologists surmise that India's history may go back 9,000 years.

No other nation on earth has a civilization that goes back as far as India's does—not even China or Egypt. The Indians are proud of their centuries-old history. At the same time, India is a modern nation that is adapting to the world as it exists now.

Westerners have known about India for centuries. The Greek conqueror Alexander the Great led his armies to the subcontinent in the year 327 BCE. During the Middle Ages, Europeans filled Indian money chests in payment for spices which were, for them, a rare and valuable commodity. Subsequently, the Portuguese, French, and finally the British built outposts in the country to expand this growing trade. During the nineteenth century, the British deposed the Indian rulers, making the country its most important colony. India finally achieved independence in 1947.

Today, the name of India often evokes the image of poverty. One third of the Indian population gets by on less than one dollar each day. In the cities, between one third and one half of the inhabitants live in slum districts, despite the fact that only three centuries ago, India was counted among the wealthiest nations in the world. In succeeding years, though, Indian rulers showed themselves incapable of modernizing the country. Colonization did more to deplete India of its riches than it did to bring progress. In addition, the rapid growth of the population has burdened the country, which must try to feed all of its citizens. As with all countries in which the population rapidly increases, there are many young people: One half of all Indians are less than eighteen years old. In these circumstances, the future of the nation is on everyone's mind.

Shubha, Jyoti, and Bhagat Invite Us to India

India's population is over one billion citizens. In other words, one out of every six human beings on earth today is Indian! Three young Indians are going to show us their country, their ways of life, and their customs.

First, there's Shubha. Her name means "full of promise." She's eleven and lives in a town in southern India called Thanjavur. She speaks Tamil. She wants to be a classical dancer. Classical dance and music go back many centuries in India, and the refinement of these arts means that prospective artists must study and practice for many years.

Jyoti's name means "light." He lives in one of the largest of the Indian cities, Calcutta, which is located in the northeast, very close to Bangladesh. He's ten and wants to work in railroad administration like his father. He already knows English, in addition to Bengali, his native language. He is quite familiar with his country, for he has traveled a lot . . . by train, of course!

Finally, Bhagat, or "the devout one," is a twelve-year-old boy whose life differs completely from that of Jyoti and Shubha. He lives in a village called Norangpur in the north of India and speaks Hindi. His parents are poor farmers. Bhagat often rebels against the life he leads. He would love to get an education, but his parents feel that schooling would serve no purpose.

Shubha, Jyoti, and Bhagat speak three different languages. They live in three regions very far from each other. Thanjavur, for example, is 1,864 miles away from Calcutta. They're part of three distinct cultures and peoples: Shubha is Tamil, Jyoti is Bengali, and Bhagat is Hindi. Nevertheless, all three consider themselves Indian first and foremost.

Shubha, the Young Tamil

Shubha lives in Thanjavur, in the state of Tamil Nadu in the southernmost part of India. Her town is famous because it contains an historic Hindu temple called the Brihadishvara. This temple, built 1,000 years ago, is so magnificent and its architecture is so extraordinary that it is famous throughout the world. It is visited by large numbers of tourists, both Indian and foreign. To pray, though, Hindus go to one of the many other temples in the city, so they won't bump into the sightseers.

 ## Shubha Gets Ready for Her Prayer Service

Yesterday evening, when she returned home from school, Shubha made cube-shaped cookies flavored with saffron. On this holiday morning, she's going to the temple with her mother to ask the gods for a favor. Her older sister, who is eighteen, has just married and would like to have a child. Her mother believes that the gods will more readily grant the young wife a child if they go to pray at the temple in their neighborhood. They go to honor the god Vishnu, who presides over successful childbirths.

Shubha gets up with the sun. She puts on the clothes that young Indian girls favor, the *salvar-kameez*—an ensemble consisting of pants (*salvar*), a blouse (*kameez*) that descends almost to the knees, and a scarf worn around the neck with long panels that reach down to the lower back.

Her mother is wearing the traditional dress of Indian women, the sari—a single piece of fabric about 19 feet long and three feet wide. Women wind the saris around their bodies. They begin by attaching them at the waist, then they cover one shoulder with the highly decorated part of the sari, the *palla*, which they throw over their backs. Under the sari, they wear a blouse that covers the shoulders completely. Shubha's mother has selected a sari woven in Varanasi, a holy city in the Indian north, on the Ganges River. Saris from Varanasi are famous and quite expensive, since they're made of silk embroidered with gold.

To finish their preparations, Shubha and her mother go to the flower stalls at the market. Indian women like to pin garlands of jasmine flowers in their long, dark hair.

Hinduism, the Religion of Most Indians

Shubha's religion is Hinduism. Over three quarters of all Indians practice Hinduism. They're called Hindus. They believe that reincarnation follows death; that is, once a person dies, he or she is reborn and returns to life in another form.

If a person has acted in a way that respects the order of the universe during his or her lifetime, if he has honored the gods or if she has worked for peace, then this individual will be reborn in a better, higher form—for example, as a sage or a priest. But if he has misdeeds and bad behavior in his life, he will be reborn in a lower form, and his next life will be hard, perhaps even disastrous. He may even live again not as a human, but as an animal or perhaps an insect. All Hindus strive, above all, to escape the cycle of reincarnation. If a person's life has been without fault, this Hindu will no longer return to earth—he'll experience "deliverance." Once "delivered" from earthly life, the individual will cease living among humans and will "dissolve" into the sphere of the divine. For Hindus, there is no paradise. They wish merely to escape human life.

Hinduism recognizes many gods, making it a polytheistic religion. However, the Hindu gods are in no way like the Greek or Roman ones who each oversaw a specific aspect of human conduct, such as war, love, wisdom, etc., and who behaved just as human beings do. On the contrary, the Hindu gods stand for ideas, or ways of existing in the universe. The two principal divinities are Vishnu and Shiva. Vishnu represents the forces that bring together or assemble, while Shiva represents the forces that disperse or destroy. This is not an antagonistic relationship, though, because these gods complement each other. The world spins and generates

because Shiva dances through the universe. In fact, statues of Shiva often depict him with multiple arms, dancing. In this way, Shiva, too, is a creator.

The Hindu gods have spouses, or *paredres* (lesser gods shown sitting beside the more powerful ones). These divinities represent the female energy, or shakti, which is of vital importance to the male gods. If there were no *paredres*, the gods would be incomplete. Hindus venerate the goddesses as much as they do the gods. Such female divinities include Kali, one of Shiva's *paredres*, and Lakshmi, the spouse of Vishnu. Goddesses, too, stand for ideas. For example, Lakshmi represents fortune. The Hindu gods can come down to earth to help humans restore the proper order of the world, especially when demons threaten those who show devotion to the gods. When Vishnu changes to human form, he becomes an avatar, a word signifying "transformation" that has a similar meaning in English. At the time of Vishnu's metamorphosis, Lakshmi accompanies him into the human world.

 ## Shubha at the Temple

In front of the temple, a sacred elephant welcomes visitors.

Each person offers him a small coin. The elephant picks it up with his trunk and gives it to his *cornac*, or caretaker. Then, very gently, the elephant lays his trunk on the shoulder of the giver. It's his way of blessing the donor. Shubha offers a coin, but she's still a little afraid when the heavy trunk is about to rest on her shoulder.

At the temple entrance, Shubha removes her sandals. Everywhere in India—in temples and at home—you have to walk barefoot to avoid spreading dirt on the floor. Nothing must come in from the outside, since such an invasion would be considered impure. Shubha heads for the innermost part of the temple where the statue of Vishnu stands. She walks around it three times; her mother insists she obey the prescribed ritual and the proper method of approach. It's a lengthy process. Many people have come, and they must wait in line. Each time her mother walks in front of the statue, she gives money to a white-robed priest, who accepts the donations to help maintain the temple.

After her third lap around the statue, Shubha opens a bag filled with the cookies she made the previous evening. She offers them to the Hindus seated cross-legged on the ground, who are either praying silently or talking among themselves. Each accepts the offering and begins eating. Through this gift, Shubha and her mother hope that the god Vishnu will grant their prayers.

Afterward, Shubha and her mother sit down. The temple reverberates with talking, and someone plays music. As time passes, others who have come to pray offer them sweets. Finally, Shubha puts her sandals back on and leaves.

Hinduism emerged several millennia ago and has changed significantly over the years. It's the oldest religion in India, but not the only one. Three other religions are also native to India.

The great promoter of Jainism, Mahavira (also called Jina), lived in the sixth century BCE. Jainism recognizes no god. As in Hinduism, a person must act so that he or she escapes the cycle of reincarnation on earth. Non-violence is an essential principle; no harm must be perpetrated against any living being, not even the smallest insect. Life is the most precious possession. At present, only 0.5 percent of Indians practice Jainism.

The Buddha created Buddhism. The Buddha was born in northern India to a princely family shortly after Mahavira's own birth in the sixth century BCE. He left his palace and shunned all luxury, power, pleasure, and gratification. He taught that in order to

achieve happiness, a person must renounce all of his or her desires. A person without desire will, after death, experience eternal repose, or nirvana. In our day, very few Buddhists remain in India, accounting for only about 0.7 percent of the population.

The Sikhs practice Panth, a religion that arose in the fifteenth century. The adherents of Panth stress the equality between women and men. There is a single god, whom humans cannot know and who, therefore, has no name. Observant Sikh men are bearded and wear turbans wound around their heads to cover their hair, which they never cut. A guru (one of the founders of the Sikh religion) made this practice mandatory. Sikh women frequently wear modern dress, such as the *salvar-kameez*. Sikhs make up about 2 percent of the Indian people, and are very numerous in the state of Punjab, in the northeast of the country.

The Parsis observe a religion that originated in Persia in the sixth century BCE and was founded by Zoroaster. There are just under one million Parsis in India. However, the Tata family, the richest family in the country, made its fortune in industry and practices Zoroastrianism.

Lastly, the Christians and Muslims of India are similar to those in other countries. They observe the same holidays, such as Christmas and Ramadan, respectively. Christians make up about 2.3 percent of the population. The followers of Islam number 130 million, or 12 percent of the people.

The Partitioning of India

Prior to 1947, when India was part of the British Empire, the percentage of Muslims in the country was much higher: 35 percent, as compared with 12 percent today.

In 1947, the British accepted the Indian demand for independence. However, the Muslims and Hindus could not reach agreement about what the Indian nation should be like following independence. The Muslims founded an independent state, which they called Pakistan, or the "country of the pure." The division of India into two countries, India and Pakistan, is called "the partition."

The Hindus living in Pakistan had to resettle in India. Also, many Muslims living in India migrated to Pakistan. That's why there are so few Indian Muslims and Pakistani Hindus.

About 14 million people left their homes during the partition. Confrontations between Hindus and Muslims caused tens of thousands of deaths. In the present day, antagonism still sparks violence between the two religions.

Shubha Wants to Become a Dancer

Shubha's father is a classical singer. He interprets the music of southern India, which is called *Carnatic* music. It's the classical music played by the Brahmins, the Indian intellectual class.

He would like his daughter to succeed at this profession. For several generations, members of

Shubha's family have been *Carnatic* singers, both male and female. Shubha studies privately with her father and her teacher, or guru. She started at the age of four. The music is elegant and intricate. Music lessons as we know them are quite different from Shubha's. There is no musical notation, with its clefs, notes, and staves. Notation wouldn't be sufficient to transcribe the nuances of the sounds of the voice and the instruments. As a result, each student must learn in ongoing collaboration with her teacher, by listening first, then trying to play, and rehearsing over and over until she knows the piece thoroughly.

Shubha can interpret many ragas (musical pieces or, more precisely, themes). A musician begins with one of these themes, then improvises versions based on various rules. She conveys to the audience a range of emotions, from joy to suffering. In a few years, if she proves herself to be really talented, Shubha may perform ragas in concert. One day she'll pass on the knowledge of *Carnatic* music to her own children.

Shubha would also like to become a dancer. From the time she was seven, Shubha has had a guru in *bharata natyam*, the classical dance of India. According to Hindu tradition, the god Shiva was the one who taught the movements of these sacred dances to humans. Each dance tells a story while following a strict code. The movements of the fingers or even of the eyes have well-defined meanings. Young girls from southern India who wish to become dancers often aspire to attend a prestigious school in the city of Madras, about 190 miles from Thanjavur. There, they learn to dance in groups under the tutelage of both male and female masters, not alone with a guru.

There are several kinds of classical music in the north and the south of India. Not only is the music itself different, but the instruments are different in each region, too. In the north, the percussion is played on a tabla, a pair of drums fitted with a single skin, tuned very precisely to give a wide variety of sounds. In the south, musicians play a *mridangam*, a high, wide drum over which two skins are stretched, one at each end, which the drummer strikes on both sides.

Shubha is aware that it's not always easy being a girl in India. A host of social differences still distinguish boys from girls, even if this gap is narrowing.

When a husband and wife are expecting a baby, they often hope for a boy. When parents marry off a daughter, they must pay a dowry to the family of the boy who marries her. The dowry is a kind of gift, but it's considered mandatory. The girl's family may offer the groom some money, a motorbike, or a few animals. Some people mistakenly claim that the dowry is the price paid for the bride, but it's the girl's parents who pay it so that the boy will marry her! Indian law outlawed the dowry system in 1961. Nevertheless, this custom has not yet disappeared entirely, especially in rural areas and in some states where progress comes more slowly than in others.

Families of modest means often have trouble paying the dowries for their daughters. As a result, poor parents try to learn the gender of their developing child early using ultrasound techniques. If the child is a girl and they expect they will lack the money to pay her dowry in the future, they sometimes choose to abort the pregnancy. This is the reason why in India today, boys outnumber girls: there are 933 girls for every 1,000 boys. If on the other hand they decide to have the girl, poor parents may go into debt to be able to pay the dowry. Normally a rich member of their village will lend them the money they need, which they will have to repay.

Frequently the lender charges an interest rate so high that the borrowers end up repaying much more than the actual sum they borrowed. Sometimes the entire family has to work to cancel the debt. This practice is called debt slavery. It's illegal, but it still happens.

The dowry does not represent the only obstacle to a happy marriage. Sometimes the young people don't get to meet each other until the day of their marriage ceremony. Some parents arrange the marriages of their children to gain a family advantage, and they know their children won't contest their decision. Arranged marriages are gradually vanishing, particularly since the legal minimum age for marriage is now eighteen. By the time they are eighteen, young people can more easily assert their own opinion and choose a mate. The custom of marrying off younger children is still observed, though, in the most destitute rural regions, and especially in Rajasthan, a state in northwestern India.

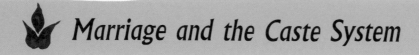

Marriage and the Caste System

The Hindu tradition imposes another marriage rule: You have to marry someone of your own "caste." Hinduism assigns human beings to a number of castes—groups of people that are separate and closed off to each other.

Not all castes have the same intrinsic worth. The very highest caste is the Brahmins—the priests, the men and women of letters, the intellectuals, and the classical musicians like Shubha and her parents. Next come the Kshatriya, or warriors and princes (or, rather, the former princes, since today there are no kings or princes who hold any power in India). The third highest caste is the Vaishya—the merchants. Then, one step lower, the Shudra includes manual laborers and servants. Finally, there are the untouchables, who belong to none of the Hindu castes and make up some 15 percent of the Indian people. Marriage to someone from a lower caste is greatly frowned on by the Hindus who follow tradition closely. However, India, like the rest of the world, is evolving, and these traditional rules are not always observed, especially in the urban areas.

Shubha knows that her parents will not force a husband on her and that she can marry whom she wants. However she does have friends who will have to marry the boys their parents choose! To her, this seems outrageous.

Shubha will also be able to choose *when* she'll marry. Since she wants to pursue her singing and dancing studies, she might not want to get married until years past her eighteenth birthday. However, most girls marry early in life, have children when still young, and devote themselves to their families and homes. Indian women work especially hard. In addition to managing their households, they frequently have to work outside the home to bring in money. Shubha might be able to lead another kind of life: singing and dancing and spreading Indian music and culture to other countries!

Priest

Intellectual

Musician

ahmins

hatriya

Soldier

Prince

shya

Merchant

udra

Manual
Laborer

Servant

touchables

Jyoti of Calcutta

Jyoti lives in Calcutta, in the northeastern part of India in the vast delta of the Ganges River. With 13 million inhabitants, it's one of the biggest cities on earth. Calcutta is a wealthy city and once even served as the capital of India. But many of the residents are stuck in shantytowns where harsh conditions prevail.

 ## Calcutta, an Immense City

During the seventeenth century, Calcutta was nothing more than a village. As a result of trade with the West, the village grew to become India's capital during the period when India belonged to the British Empire. During the Colonial era, the British ruled India on their own, as all Indians were kept away from political power. In Calcutta and throughout the region of Bengal, the Indians fought against the colonizers in a campaign to expel them from the country. In 1912, as a punishment for their rebellion, the British decided to transfer the capital from Calcutta to Delhi. Even after the advent of independence in 1947, Delhi remained the capital, and Calcutta lost a great deal of its political importance.

Today, Calcutta is infamous for its destitute neighborhoods and slums. These districts, which harbor families struggling in poverty and deprivation, extend over vast, overcrowded areas, lack running water, and suffer a range of other problems. Yet it's in these neighborhoods that communities flourish. Indian women go out each day to combat their poverty by setting up credit networks on a collective basis. They pool their small savings which, when poured into a common treasury, can give aid to the most needy among them.

Jyoti lives in a sixth-floor apartment in a building in central Calcutta. Each morning before sunrise, his mother wakes Jyoti and his older brother from their shared bedroom, and their two sisters in another.

Everyone washes, then they all have breakfast in the British style: big cups of tea with milk, cereal, and, on occasion, slices of bread. Then they all drink glasses of fruit juice. Their father leaves for his office, Jyoti's brother goes off to the university, and the three other children head for their school. Jyoti's mother stays at home to work. She translates articles into English for British and American magazines.

Each morning, Jyoti and his two sisters hail a rickshaw to travel to their school, which is fairly far from home. A rickshaw is a sort of carriage drawn by a bicycle. Because of its low cost, the rickshaw is a popular way to travel. For Jyoti, it's much less tiring than walking. It may seem strange to us to sit and be pulled by a man who pedals his bike, but it's normal in India. For a long time, men running on foot pulled the rickshaws. This was an especially grueling trade, since the rickshaw drivers had to expend a lot of energy weaving among the hordes of cars, trucks, and buses, in terrible heat. It proved particularly painful during the monsoon season. At that time, rain falls in massive torrents all over India. It's a meteorological phenomenon that strikes in only a few tropical regions, but in India—especially Calcutta—it is quite extraordinary. The city lies at the southern end of the Himalaya mountains, which form a barrier that channels heat and rainfall onto the plain.

The monsoon season lasts from July to September. During these months, up to 40 feet of water can fall within a few weeks! Yet the monsoons are vital for agriculture and, as a result, for the entire nation.

After all, the more than one billion inhabitants of India have to eat. On the other hand, the assaults of wind and rain can paralyze the major cities, especially the transportation systems.

Trains are the most widely used form of transportation for long trips. The Indian railroads are especially important because the country is so vast and very few people own a car. Jyoti's father is employed here at the railroad administration. The British began construction of the rail network, which is Asia's largest with 38,000 miles of track.

Indians travel a great deal, from their villages to the city, for example, or to make religious pilgrimages to holy spots like Varanasi on the Ganges River. Jyoti and his family often go by train to Darjeeling, which is about 375 miles from Calcutta. Darjeeling, a small city in the Himalayas, is renowned for the tea it produces—some of the best in the world. Jyoti's parents appreciate its cooler climate, and the train ride is among the most spectacular on earth. This particular rail line, first built in 1881, rises in the space of just a few miles to an altitude of more than 6,500 feet through the breathtaking Himalayan landscapes.

The People of Calcutta Speak Bengali

At Jyoti's school, classes are taught in Bengali, the language of the region of Bengal (an area that includes Calcutta and Bangladesh). Bengali belongs to the Indo-European family of languages.

As the name implies, the Indo-European group contains the languages spoken in India and Europe. All of these languages spring from a very old source: Sanskrit, an Indian language several millennia old. A lot of words we use in English derive from ancient cultures. A large number of Latin words came from ancient Greek, which, in turn, borrowed an important part of its vocabulary from Sanskrit. Although Bengali and English are written using different alphabets, they both derive from a single, very ancient origin.

Jyoti is also learning English. He thinks it's a convenient way to communicate with other Indians who speak different languages. There are so many languages spoken in India, a person can't learn them all! About 150 million people speak Bengali, so it's one of the nation's most important languages after Hindi, another Indo-European language spoken by 300–400 million people in the north of India. In the south, the languages are part of the Dravidian family. The most common of these is Tamil, Shubha's native tongue.

The Dravidian and Indo-European languages differ completely—even the sentence construction is totally different. As you can imagine, this doesn't make communication any easier between the north and south of the country. To speak to one another, the upper classes of society resort to the colonizers' language, English. If, for example, Shubha wanted to write to Jyoti, she'd have to do it in English! It's also the language in which many newspapers are written, and it allows Indians to communicate fluently with foreign nations. There are many more people in the world who speak English than who speak Hindi or Tamil.

This means that many children in India are bilingual. They speak their own language and English, too.

Long Live Bollywood!

Only 40 percent of all Indians have televisions at home. They would rather go out to the movies. It's the least expensive form of entertainment, and much cheaper than concerts of Indian classical music or dance. You can find movie houses even in India's small towns.

A surprising fact: India is the biggest movie producer in the world, surpassing even the United States! Each year, the Indian film industry turns out about 900 movies. Playing off the similarity to the United States' Hollywood, movie fans use the nickname "Bollywood" for the Indian movie studios. The largest of these, which are located in Bombay, Calcutta, and Madras, make movies in the many Indian languages.

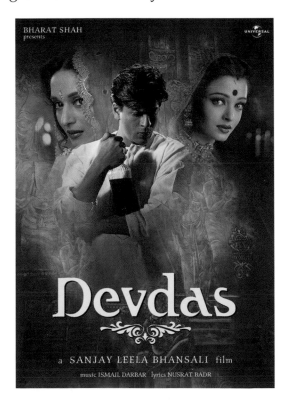

Indian movies differ greatly from our own. Like Western films, they tell stories of love, friendship, or conflict. But they often cover historical subjects, such as the life of the Buddhist emperor Ashoka, who lived more than 2,000 years ago, or the drama of the Partition, which forms the backdrop for stories of friendship—or hatred—between Muslims and Hindus. And during the three- or four-hour running times, the actors sing and dance. When the leading actor appears on the screen, the moviegoers scream their hearts out!

What Do Indians Eat?

Throughout the north, wheat is the main food staple. It's made into chapatis, or small, flat rounds made of water and flour—like bread.

Because Calcutta is such a large city and his school is far from his home, Jyoti eats lunch in the cafeteria. In the evening, his mother prepares a traditional Indian meal. She buys ready-made chapatis, as opposed to in the countryside, where people bake them each day on plates suspended over wood fires. They are eaten with vegetables and sauces that are seasoned with peppers, according to taste.

The main component of the meal is rice. India is one of the world's leading producers of rice. In the south, rice is eaten at every meal, either in grain form accompanied by dozens of different sauces, or as a flour, which is mixed with other flours to make a whole range of dishes. For example, southerners eat *dosa*, large pancakes made of rice and chickpea flours filled with cooked potatoes, and *idli*, little steamed balls of rice and lentils.

India is a country of spices. Jyoti absolutely loves them. There are all kinds of spices, some of which we use here, too: anise, cinnamon, cumin, cloves, mustard,

and pepper. Others, though, are used specifically for Indian cooking, including cardamom, turmeric (which has an orange-yellow color), and nigella, which is used for cooking vegetables. Jyoti's mother buys prepared curry at a spice market where dozens of varieties are sold. But many women make it at home by mixing a number of spices: capsicum, mustard, cumin, curry leaves, and turmeric, for color.

After the meal, Jyoti munches on *betel*, the thick leaf of a pepper plant that grows in India. These leaves are filled with various ingredients, such as the areca nut, which is found locally. They're sold on the street by specialized merchants. Chewing *betel* produces a vivid red saliva that people spit out on the sidewalk—an odd custom from our point of view, yet it really helps digestion!

MADURAI MEENAKSHI
APPALAM & CHIPS

Eau de Rose

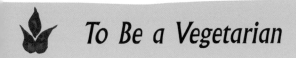

To Be a Vegetarian

In India, meals are very different than what we're used to. First of all, Indians eat without knives and forks. Instead, they use the fingers of their right hands. The left is considered impure and must never touch the food.

Some foods are considered impure. According to this belief, these foods are not in harmony with the order of the universe and with the pattern of behavior that each person must adopt. Religion prohibits them. For example, a Hindu wishing to act so as to preserve the harmony of the world never eats meat because, Hinduism says, you must not harbor the "desire to kill." This trait is termed *ahimsa*. So there's only one solution: Be a vegetarian.

Hindu vegetarians eat grains, vegetables, fruits, milk, and ghi, a clarified butter. To make up for the absence of meat and fish, Indians have created all kinds of dishes that mimic meat's consistency. For example, by mixing together green bananas, mangoes, spices, and cheese, you get a paste that tastes and feels something like fish. In this way, vegetarian chefs have produced one of the most sophisticated cuisines in the world. Generally speaking, the members of the higher castes are the ones who follow a vegetarian diet, an observance that represents one more step toward deliverance. Since the members of the lower castes have further to go to achieve deliverance, they are less reluctant to eat meat.

Like all Indians, Jyoti loves tea, which is infused directly into milk. In food stalls everywhere, sellers heat tea at low boil. For a few paise, you can buy a hot cup of tea. For a little more money, there's lassi, another thirst-quencher made of yogurt and milk, with a few drops of rose water added.

Bhagat,
a Young "Untouchable"

Bhagat is twelve. He lives in a village in northern India called Norangpur. Like Bhagat, most Indians live in the countryside. There are about 700 million who live in rural areas, as compared to the 300 million who live in the cities. And like all of the other Indian villages, Norangpur is split down the middle. The "upper castes" live in one part. The "untouchables" live in the other.

 ## Bhagat's Village

Bhagat's house is very humble. It's built of cob, a mixture of earth and straw. The roof is sheet metal. Bhagat's father hopes to build a real roof overlaid with tiles one day. There's only a single room—an environment that's not especially pleasant, neither for the parents, who have no privacy, nor for Bhagat himself, who must do his schoolwork with the background noise of his parents and his younger brother and sister. He sleeps in a traditional bed, a *charpai*, made of ropes strung over an unadorned wood frame with four feet. In the dry season, when it's very hot and no rain falls, Bhagat frequently sleeps outside, since it's cooler and more comfortable.

During the monsoon season, though, so much rain falls that the water always manages to get through one or two holes in the roof. Bhagat is careful to keep his schoolbooks dry. Although the monsoon season is not his favorite, he's well aware that it is important for his father and for all of India's farmers. To ensure that the harvest will be good, they need enough water to make the rice grow, but not so much that the crops rot before ripening.

In Norangpur, the villagers are farmers. Bhagat's father owns a tiny patch of land, a buffalo, and a few goats. His family lives in poverty, as do the vast majority of the farmers. Every year hundreds of thousands of farmers go to the most populous cities, where they hope survival will be easier than in the countryside. Often, they lose their jobs or are forced to sell the fields they had cultivated to repay their debts. Bhagat's father is adamant in his decision to stay in the village.

Bhagat has already traveled to Delhi, the capital, but, like his father, he prefers rural life. In Delhi he saw people piled up in extensive shantytowns and huddled in their homes, which are thrown together with sheet metal and plastic tarps. Bhagat does not envy the children mired in poverty in the city, who must work to survive. At least in Norangpur, he has a real house. He can play with his friends and go to school. At the same time, though, Bhagat has not been touched by the same good fortune as Shubha and Jyoti. He belongs to a specific group, the *chamars*, which has determined much of his family's fate.

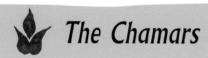 ## The Chamars

In India, every individual is defined by the caste system. Some people belong to the religious castes: Brahmins, Kshatriya, Vaishya, or Shudra. Yet even many Indians who are considered Hindu are not in any of these four castes.

In the past, these Indians were called "untouchables." Indians who belong to the caste system consider contact with them to be impure, like touching food with one's left hand.

Purity is an essential social underpinning in India. It has nothing to do with cleanliness. If you wash your hands, you may be clean but not necessarily pure. Purity requires that you observe the proper order of the universe, the dharma. For example, you must not use violence, you

must be a vegetarian, you must refrain from touching dirty or dead things, and so on. But those people who have no caste are not allowed to disturb the dharma. So they perform work that the Hindus in the caste system cannot undertake because it's judged to be impure. The untouchables help the caste-bound Hindus remain as pure as possible, by sparing them all contact with impure objects, such as animal grease, dirty laundry, or leather. Since contact with leather, a substance derived from a dead animal, is thought to be impure, one group of untouchables has devoted itself to working leather. These are the *chamars*.

In India, human beings are also classified according to profession.

The *chamars* make up one job-related caste—but there are many, many more. Here again, classification imposes a ranking system that is precisely worked out. The "purer" the profession, the higher the esteem given to it. In this way, there are castes of leather workers, of fishermen, of launderers, and so forth. No Indian can change his or her caste and, in accordance with tradition, he may eat only with Indians whose castes have a status equal to his own.

41

In his village, Bhagat must always let children of the higher castes pass in front of him. An invisible boundary separates the *chamar* neighborhood from that of the upper caste, and it can only be crossed for specific jobs, such as cleaning the streets or carrying off a corpse.

Running counter to tradition, though, present-day Indian law forbids anything that highlights the "untouchable" status of a person. No one has the right to prohibit an untouchable from drawing water from a well because they would make the well water impure. Untouchables may also attend temple, even though they were forbidden to do so for centuries. And yet they're still stigmatized by society. For this reason, they no longer wish to be called "untouchables," but rather *dalit*, which means "oppressed" in another of the Indian languages, Marathi.

The Status of the Dalits *in India*

Little by little, the *dalits* are banding together and gaining various rights. They receive positions set aside for them in the government. This practice is termed "affirmative action," meaning assistance provided to someone belonging to a disadvantaged group.

The *dalits* have their own political parties, which are energized and influential in some regions in India. The nation even had a *dalit* president from 1997 to 2002. Some of the members of this class, including a few movie actors, have become rich and famous. At home, Bhagat has hung the portrait of the most famous Indian *dalit*, Babasaheb Ambedkar. Ambedkar, who died in 1956, was the Indian Minister of Justice after India achieved independence. He fought his entire life for the rights of the untouchables. Much remains to be done before the *dalits* are treated

with equality. The newspapers frequently report crimes that are committed against the *dalits* merely because they are not included in the caste system. The upper castes despise and insult them and beat them—sometimes to death. Bhagat wants to become an attorney so that he can defend the *dalits*.

 ## Bhagat Goes to School

Bhagat knows that only by studying will he be able to improve his life. Less than a century ago, he wouldn't have been allowed to get an education. Now, however, universities have set aside places for the *dalits*, and Bhagat plans to earn one of these spots when he's finished with high school.

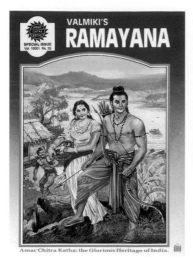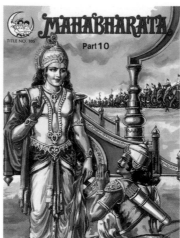

Amar Chitra Katha: the Glorious Heritage of India.

Since India lacks the resources to build schools everywhere in the country, teachers and students scramble to arrange things as best they can. When he was small, Bhagat attended the village school. The teacher taught beneath a massive banyan tree. The children sat cross-legged under the tree, listening to the lesson. There, Bhagat learned to write with chalk on a slate board. Now all of the children from each nearby village attend the same school, both the untouchables and the kids from the upper castes, but they keep their distance from each other. The teacher in Norangpur, Bhagat's village, comes from the upper caste. To supplement his meager salary, he asks the *dalit* kids to bring him things like flour, lentils, and rice. On the other hand, no food prepared by the *chamar* women is allowed—it is, from his point of view, impure.

Bhagat is a good student. When he was ten, he left for the neighboring town to continue school. The school there has several classrooms, walls, a strong roof, learning materials, and a teacher who receives a salary from the government. Bhagat can forget about bringing the teacher rice! Every evening, he returns on foot to Norangpur, about 2.5 miles away. Bhagat takes courses in Hindi, the language of his region. Next year, he'll start learning English, which is the language used in the university. He'll have to work very hard to maintain his grades.

What Subjects Are Taught in School?

In India, education is free and unrestricted for children under the age of fourteen. Still, girls have a lower literacy level than boys, since some parents believe that education for girls is unnecessary.

Some young girls do nothing but help their mothers at home. Roughly 75 percent of boys are literate (they know how to read and write), as compared to only 54 percent of girls. Gradually, though, the percentage of literate Indians, both girls and boys, is increasing.

In Indian schools, as in schools throughout the world, coursework includes mathematics, history, geography, and science. Not all Indian children learn in the same language. No matter what language they speak, though, all of them read a few highly important texts, in particular the epics written centuries ago. The two most famous are the *Ramayana* and the *Mahabharata*. The first is the story of the god Vishnu when he came down to earth as human (in the form of a prince named Rama). His wife, Sita, was kidnapped by a demon, and the *Ramayana* tells how Rama rescues Sita. The *Mahabharata* describes a battle between two warring clans that took place thousands of years ago. This epic poem also provides information about the Indian world, religion, and the state of knowledge of that time, among other things.

Other Children Have to Work

Many Indian children must work in order to live. The Indian government calculates that there are at least 11 million working children, but according to the International Labor Organization, an agency of the United Nations, that number may actually exceed 40 million.

Bhagat may be poor, but he is not forced to work. But this is not true of many other children in India. They make carpets and saris, candles, matches, bidis (a kind of small cigarette), and other products. They have jobs that threaten their health, for example in the glass and diamond trades, where great volumes of dust cause serious diseases of the skin, eyes, and other parts of the body. None of these children go to school. In 1933, the government prohibited child labor under the age of fifteen. But India's economy has not made it possible to give every adult a job that pays enough, and so the most destitute parents have no other choice—they must put their children to work. The salary they earn, while almost negligible, does allow them to eat. The most ominous part of all this is that child labor in India is not decreasing at all.

There's More to Life Than School!

Bhagat's village has no movie theater, but there are other distractions: wandering street singers, storytellers, dancers, acrobats, and even snake charmers ply their trades from village to village.

These performers are paid by the members of the village. Popular music and dance are completely different from the classical ragas that Shubha

learns. It's the same difference we see here between classical and folk music. For example, the village dancers' costumes are much simpler that the ones worn by the *bharata natyam* troupes. And their songs tell stories about working in the fields, the changing seasons, or marriage and love.

In all parts of India, from north to south, people celebrate a lot of holidays. Like all young Indians, Shubha, Jyoti, and Bhagat love the festivals. Shubha especially adores the festival of Divali, the festival of lights dedicated to the goddess Lakshmi. On that day, Indians light millions of flickering lamps and ignite firecrackers. Large parades are held, with enormous floats. But Bhagat prefers the rural festivals that mark the changing seasons. The most important of these is Holi, which falls at the end of the cold season. Everyone paints his or her face and wears colorful clothes. During this holiday, you can't tell who belongs to which caste! There are also festivals in honor of the various gods and goddesses, and then those celebrated by the Muslims and the Sikhs, and many other non-religious holidays.

Photographic Credits:

Cover: © Thierry Chantegret
p. 6: © Getty Images/Robert Harding World Imagery
p. 15: © CORBIS/Chris Lisle
p. 21: © CORBIS/Lindsay Hebberd
p. 23: © CORBIS/Galen Rowell
p. 29: © Getty Images/Robert Harding World Imagery
pp. 30–31: © CORBIS/Jeremy Horner
p. 41: © CORBIS/Jeremy Horner
p. 43: © CORBIS/Vince Streano
p. 47: © CORBIS/Lindsay Hebberd

Library of Congress Cataloging-in-Publication Data has been applied for.
ISBN 10: 0-8109-5736-1
ISBN 13: 978-0-8109-5736-7

copyright © 2006 Éditions de la Martinière Jeunesse, Paris
English translation copyright © 2006 Harry N. Abrams, Inc.

Printed and bound in France
by Pollina - n° L40237 A
10 9 8 7 6 5 4 3 2 1

HNA
harry n. abrams, inc.
a subsidiary of La Martinière Groupe
115 West 18th Street
New York, NY 10011
www.hnabooks.com